COMBAT CONTROLLERS

by Kim Covert

Consultant:
Robert V. Martens, Jr.
Senior Master Sergeant
23rd Special Tactics Squadron

CAPSTONE BOOKS

an imprint of Capstone Press
Mankato, Minnesota

Capstone Books are published by Capstone Press
151 Good Counsel Drive, P. O. Box 669, Mankato, Minnesota 56002
http://www.capstone-press.com

Library of Congress Cataloging-in-Publication Data
Covert, Kim.
    U.S. Air Force Special Forces: Combat controllers/by Kim Covert.
    p. cm.—(Warfare and weapons)
    Includes bibliographical references (p. 44) and index.
    Summary: An introduction to the Air Force Special Forces Combat controllers,
their history and development, missions, training, and equipment.
    ISBN 0-7368-0334-3
    1. United States. Air Force—Combat controllers—Juvenile literature.
[1. United States. Air Force—Combat controllers.] I. Title. II. Series.
    UG703.C68 2000
    358.4—dc21   99-27334
                                                                             CIP

Editorial Credits
Blake Hoena, editor; Timothy Halldin, cover designer; Linda Clavel, illustrator;
    Heidi Schoof, photo researcher

Photo Credits
Corbis, 36
Corbis/Bettmann, 15
Corbis/Hulton-Deutsch Collection, 17
Defense Visual Information Center, 4, 7, 8, 12, 20, 23, 24, 28, 30, 32, 39, 41, 45
Photri-Microstock, cover

Table of Contents

Features

Chapter 1

Combat Controllers

On October 3, 1993, Somalian soldiers shot down two U.S. Army Blackhawk helicopters. These helicopters crashed in Mogadishu, Somalia. They were carrying troops sent to capture a group of Somalian warlords. These military leaders had been responsible for attacks against the Somalian people. Somalian soldiers then attacked the U.S. troops aboard the crashed helicopters.

The U.S. military sent a team of soldiers to rescue the troops. Combat Controller SSgt. Jeffrey Bray was part of this team. Bray set up radio communications with U.S. gunships. He helped direct these aircrafts' crews to shoot at

U.S. soldiers in Somalia were traveling in Blackhawk helicopters like this one.

the Somalian soldiers. The gunships protected the U.S. troops until they were rescued.

"First There"

Combat Controllers (CCTs) are specially trained members of the U.S. Air Force (USAF). CCTs establish assault zones. U.S. forces use these areas in hostile territory to carry out military missions. CCTs prepare assault zones for incoming aircraft. These aircraft may be sent to attack enemy forces or to perform rescue missions.

CCTs set up landing zones. They find safe places for aircraft to land. CCTs often use enemy airfields for landing zones. They sometimes use explosives to remove obstacles from landing areas. They may blow up vehicles or other objects that are on runways.

CCTs also set up drop zones. They locate safe areas for parachutists to land. Parachutists jump out of aircraft over drop zones. These soldiers wear parachutes when they jump. These large pieces of strong, lightweight cloth allow soldiers to float safely to the ground.

Combat Controllers set up landing zones for aircraft.

CCTs often are among the first soldiers sent on a mission. CCTs have a motto for the duties they perform. This saying is "First There." CCTs perform duties that help other U.S. military groups arrive safely in enemy territory. CCTs locate assault zones. They inform friendly forces about the assault zones. This information may include weather conditions, enemy locations, or the best direction to approach an assault zone.

Combat Controllers set up drop zones for parachutists.

Air Force Special Operations Command

Combat Controllers are part of the U.S. Air Force Special Operations Command (AFSOC). Members of AFSOC perform special operations missions. Most air force members are not trained to perform these missions.

Special operations missions often are secret and dangerous. They may involve sneaking into enemy territory. Some missions are planned to destroy enemy military headquarters. Others may involve rescuing pilots whose aircraft have been shot down in enemy territory.

Communications

Combat Controllers are in charge of air traffic control in assault zones. They guide military aircraft in and out of these areas. CCTs use portable beacons that allow pilots to locate assault zones. These beacons send light signals to pilots.

CCTs radio other information to pilots. They tell pilots about weather conditions in assault zones. CCTs tell pilots when to have parachutists jump out of their aircraft. This helps parachutists land in the drop zones. CCTs also direct aircraft crews where to shoot at enemy forces.

CCTs provide communications during missions. They set up air-to-ground radios. These radios allow aircraft pilots to talk with military commanders on the ground. CCTs also set up satellite radios for long distance communications. These radios send signals through spacecraft orbiting the Earth. These radios allow rear headquarters' commanders to communicate with mission members. These commanders are not at assault zones. Instead, they help guide missions from their headquarters. Their headquarters may be in another country.

Special Tactics Teams

Combat Controllers often work with Pararescuemen (PJs) during special operations missions. PJs perform search-and-rescue missions. PJs often help pilots whose aircraft have crashed. They carry medical equipment and know how to treat injured people.

PJs and CCTs work together on Special Tactics Teams (STTs) to perform their missions. STTs often are the first group to take part in special operations missions. CCTs set up assault zones and air traffic control systems. PJs prepare to perform rescue operations and to treat soldiers injured during missions. CCTs and PJs support each other in their duties.

Blue background:
stands for the U.S.
Air Force

Lightning bolt: stands
for communication; it
also stands for how
quickly CCTs can
carry out their
missions.

Parachute: stands for
one of the main
ways CCTs
reach assault
zones

FIRST THERE

U.S.A.F. COMBAT CONTROL

Silver background:
stands for aircraft

Compass rose:
stands for the
work CCTs do all
around the world

11

Chapter 2

History

The history of Combat Controllers began during World War II (1939–1945). During this war, the United States fought on the side of the Allied nations. This group of countries included Canada, the United Kingdom, France, and Russia. The Allied nations were at war with the Axis powers. These nations included Germany, Japan, and Italy.

U.S. soldiers often parachuted to assault zones to perform missions. Parachutists had many challenges during these missions. Aircraft pilots sometimes got lost or flew into bad weather. The pilots then could not find the assault zones. Parachutists sometimes landed 30 miles (48 kilometers) or more from their drop zones.

During World War II, pilots sometimes had trouble flying parachutists over assault zones.

Pathfinders

Military leaders realized they needed people on the ground to help guide aircraft. They organized and trained a small group of parachutists. They called these parachutists Pathfinders. Pathfinders were trained to arrive ahead of the main military forces. They then would help guide aircraft pilots to assault zones.

Pathfinders used several methods to communicate with pilots. Pathfinders used high-powered lights to signal aircraft pilots. They also used flares and smoke pots. These devices produced bright light or smoke to show pilots the location of drop zones. Pathfinders also sent information about weather conditions to pilots by radio.

In September 1943, Pathfinders carried out their first mission. The U.S. Army planned to airdrop Allied troops in Italy. These troops were from countries friendly to the United States. They would help soldiers already fighting in Italy. Pathfinders parachuted into the area to set

During World War II, Pathfinders would arrive before the main airborne force parachuted in.

up drop zones for Allied troops. They arrived only minutes before the main airborne forces. Pathfinders helped successfully guide these aircraft over drop zones.

In 1947, the military formed the U.S. Air Force as a separate branch of the military. Before, the air force had been part of the army. It was called the U.S. Army Air Forces (AAF).

The new USAF formed its own Pathfinder teams in 1953. Later that year, the USAF renamed these teams Combat Control Teams. CCTs provided air traffic control for aircraft in combat areas.

The Vietnam and Gulf Wars

Combat Controllers performed many missions during the Vietnam War (1954–1975). CCTs provided air traffic control during hundreds of airlift missions. CCTs helped safely guide aircraft transporting soldiers to assault zones. They also helped aircraft pilots locate targets on bombing missions.

CCTs also played an important role during the Gulf War (1991). In August 1990, Iraq's army attacked Kuwait. The U.S. military then sent troops to nearby Saudi Arabia. The U.S. military hoped to prevent Iraq's army from attacking other countries. CCTs provided air traffic control for many of the aircraft arriving in Saudi Arabia.

In January 1991, the United States and its allies attacked Iraq. Pilots bombed Iraqi

During the Vietnam War, Combat Controllers helped direct aircraft transporting troops to assault zones.

targets. These sites included military headquarters and anti-aircraft weapons. Iraq used anti-aircraft weapons to shoot at U.S. aircraft. Pilots also transported ground troops and supplies to battle sites. CCTs helped the pilots perform these missions.

Mission

Operation: Urgent Fury

Date: October 24, 1983

Location: Point Salines Airfield, Grenada

Combat Controllers: Teams of CCTs boarded five MC-130 airplanes at Hurlburt Field, Florida. These aircraft then flew to Hunter Army Airfield, Georgia. There, the CCTS received instructions for their mission. U.S. Army Rangers also boarded these planes at Hunter Airfield.

Point Salines Airfield: A group of 41 Rangers and 12 CCTs parachuted from one of the MC-130s. They landed at the airfield. The CCTs quickly set up air-to-ground radio communications for incoming aircraft.

Enemy Fire: Rebel forces fired at the CCTs. The CCTs radioed AC-130 Gunships circling over the airfield. They helped guide these airplanes' crews to fire at the enemy troops.

Air Traffic Control: CCTs provided air traffic control for aircraft flying into Point Salines Airfield. They helped safely guide aircraft carrying troops and supplies to the airfield. Within a few days, U.S. forces had defeated the rebels.

Point Salines

18

Kilometers
0 1 2 3
☆ Capital
0 1 2
Miles

Caribbean
Sea

GRENADA

☆ St. George's

Atlantic
Ocean

North
America

Atlantic
Ocean

Pacific
Ocean

South
America

Chapter 3

Training

Combat Controllers are highly qualified members of the U.S. Air Force. They must be physically and mentally fit. They must be able to learn many special skills. These skills include parachuting and how to use air traffic control equipment. Very few people are able to complete CCT training.

Airmen

Both men and women can volunteer for the USAF. These people must be between 17 and 27 years old. They must be high school graduates and in good health. The USAF calls these volunteers airmen. But only men can become Combat Controllers. Congressional law does not allow women to enter ground combat specialties.

Combat Controllers must be physically fit.

These jobs involve duties that are performed while under direct fire from enemy forces.

Airmen who want to enter CCT training must first pass a difficult physical fitness test. They must swim, run, and perform other exercises. Airmen must be strong, dedicated, and physically fit to pass this test.

The Training Pipeline

Airmen who pass the physical test enter the training pipeline. These trainees attend training at eight schools. Their training lasts for about one year.

The first school in the pipeline is at Lackland Air Force Base (AFB), Texas. Training at this school involves the Pararescue/Combat Control Indoctrination Course. This course consists of physical and mental conditioning. Trainees swim, run, and lift weights. They also learn the history of Combat Controllers. The course is challenging. About 70 percent of trainees do not finish it.

Trainees next attend the U.S. Army Airborne School and the U.S. Army Combat Divers

Combat Controllers learn to use scuba gear at Combat Divers School.

School. The Airborne School is at Fort Benning, Georgia. Trainees learn basic parachuting skills at this school. Combat Divers School is in Key West, Florida. Trainees learn how to use scuba gear at this school. Scuba stands for self-contained underwater breathing apparatus. This is a difficult course for many trainees. CCTs wearing scuba gear may have to carry up to 170 pounds (77 kilograms) of equipment.

Combat Controller trainees must learn to parachute.

Trainees next attend U.S. Navy Underwater Egress Training at Pensacola Naval Air Station (NAS), Florida. Trainees learn how to escape from sinking aircraft here.

Trainees then attend the USAF Basic Survival School at Fairchild AFB, Washington. At this school, they learn survival skills that help them stay alive in the wilderness. They learn how to survive in jungles, woods, mountains, and other remote areas. They also learn ways to hide from enemy forces and return to safety.

The U.S. Army Military Free Fall Parachutist School is at the Yuma Proving Grounds in Arizona. Trainees learn HALO parachuting skills at this school. HALO stands for "high altitude, low opening." People also call this method of parachuting free fall parachuting. HALO parachuting involves jumping from an aircraft at a very high distance above the ground. But the parachutist opens the parachute much closer to the ground. Parachutists may jump from an altitude of more than 30,000 feet (9,144 meters). They may open their parachutes as low as 3,500 feet (1,067 meters) above the ground. This method of parachuting makes it difficult for enemy forces to see the parachutist.

Trainees next attend the Air Traffic Control Operator Course at Keesler AFB, Mississippi. Trainees learn air traffic control skills in this course.

Combat Control School is the final school in the pipeline. This school is at Pope AFB, North Carolina. Trainees here work on all the skills they will use as CCTs. They also learn to work with beacons and other communications equipment. In this school, CCTs learn how to locate and set up assault zones. They learn the rules and procedures for safely guiding aircraft in and out of assault zones. They learn how to establish radio communication and provide air traffic control instructions to pilots. They also learn to work with dynamite and other explosives that may be needed to clear landing areas.

Graduates of this school earn a scarlet beret. This hat shows that they have finished CCT training. Now they are qualified to be CCT apprentices. These beginning CCTs then will train under more experienced CCTs.

Training never ends for CCTs. Some learn to become parachute jumpmasters or scuba-dive supervisors. These instructors train other people to parachute or scuba dive. Other CCTs may test new aircraft or parachutes. CCTs also learn how to use new radio and air traffic equipment.

Military Terms

AAF – Army Air Forces

AFSOC – Air Force Special Operations Command

CCT – Combat Controller

clipper – dishwashing equipment in air force dining halls

hooyah – a word spoken by a person who agrees with what someone is saying

grunt – a member of the U.S. Army

jarhead – a member of the U.S. Marines

pathfinders – the first combat controllers

PJ – Pararescueman

rainbows – airmen arriving at basic training in brightly colored civilian clothing

rotorheads – U.S. Air Force helicopter pilots

STT – Special Tactic Team

training pipeline – a training program for Combat Controllers

tailpipes – a radio name for Combat Controllers during the Vietnam War

USAF – U.S. Air Force

Chapter 4

Vehicles and Equipment

Combat Controllers perform missions all around the world. They use many methods to reach assault zones. They may jump out of airplanes. They may travel by boat. They may climb mountains. The USAF provides the vehicles and equipment that CCTs need to complete their missions.

Parachutes

Combat Controllers usually travel in aircraft to their mission sites. CCTs most often use the C-130 airplane to travel. This large cargo plane can transport up to 92 combat troops.

Combat Controllers often travel in C-130 aircraft.

Special Tactic Teams often use helicopters during rescue missions.

Troops parachute out of the C-130's side doors over drop zones.

CCTs are trained to parachute from aircraft. They use the HALO method of parachuting when jumping from planes at high altitudes. At low altitudes, CCTs often use static-line parachutes. The static line is a cord attached from the parachute to the aircraft. It pulls the parachute open as soon as the CCT jumps.

Helicopters

Combat Controllers often must reach areas where airplanes cannot fly. Helicopters sometimes transport CCTs to these areas. The USAF uses MH-60 Pave Hawk helicopters for many special operations missions. The USAF also uses the MH-53J Pave Low III helicopter for special operations. It is the USAF's largest and most powerful helicopter.

STTs use helicopters on rescue missions and to reach assault zones. Their helicopters are equipped to transport injured people. They can fly well at night and in bad weather. This allows STTs to carry out their missions quickly and safely.

Land and Sea

Combat Controllers are trained to use many other types of vehicles to reach assault zones. They also may ride motorcycles to reach assault zones. They may use snowmobiles to travel across snowy areas. They may drive all-terrain vehicles (ATVs). These vehicles can travel over

rough, bumpy ground. ATVs can be used to carry equipment such as radios and beacons to assault zones.

CCTs must start some missions over the ocean. They often use HALO parachuting for jumps over water. They also may drop inflatable Zodiac boats by parachute. These rubber boats fill with air. Zodiacs are equipped with engines. CCTs use Zodiacs to reach land. CCTs usually use these boats at night so the enemy cannot spot them.

Equipment and Weapons

Combat Controllers usually carry more than 80 pounds (36 kilograms) of equipment on missions. CCTs use this equipment to perform their duties. CCTs use some of their equipment to perform air traffic control duties. They use many types of radios for communications. They use special navigational equipment to provide pilots with directions to assault zones. They carry lights to place along landing zones. These lights help pilots know where to land their

All-terrain vehicles help Combat Controllers reach assault zones.

aircraft. CCTs also use flare guns to send signals to pilots.

Most special operations missions take place at night. CCTs wear night vision goggles for these missions. The goggles use light from the moon and stars to help CCTs see at night.

CCTs also may wear oxygen equipment for HALO parachuting. People cannot breathe easily at high altitudes. There is not enough oxygen for them to breathe.

CCTs sometimes carry rappelling equipment. This rope-climbing equipment allows CCTs to climb down steep hillsides. CCTs also use rappelling equipment to lower themselves from helicopters.

CCTs carry weapons to protect themselves. The M-4 carbine rifle is the most common weapon CCTs carry. This automatic assault rifle can fire bullets rapidly. CCTs also can add a flashlight or grenade launcher to this rifle. Grenades are small explosives.

Important Dates

1939 – World War II begins

1943 – U.S. Army Pathfinders carry out their first mission by guiding aircraft over drop zones in Italy

1947 – U.S. Air Force becomes a separate branch of the military

1953 – U.S. Air Force forms the first combat control teams

1954 – Vietnam War begins

1981 – MH-53J Pave Low III first used

1983 – Operation Urgent Fury; CCTs parachute to Point Salines Airfield in Grenada. They set up air-to-ground radio communications and provide air traffic control.

1989 – Operation Just Cause; CCTs parachute to Rio Hato and Torrios Tocumen Airfields in Panama. They set up air-to-ground radio communications and provide air traffic control.

1991 – Gulf War; CCTs provide air traffic control around airfields during the war.

1994 – M-4 carbine rifle first used

Chapter 5

Present and Future

Combat Controllers train and perform missions even during peacetime. They carry out humanitarian missions. CCTs perform these missions to help people in need.

CCTs continue to train during peacetime. They hold training missions with members of other military groups. They also demonstrate their skills at special performances. CCTs remain prepared to enter combat at any time.

Operation Provide Comfort

Combat Controllers provide air traffic control for humanitarian missions around

Humanitarian missions help people around the world.

the world. One such mission was Operation Provide Comfort.

After the Gulf War, thousands of Kurds left their homes in northern Iraq. These people did not want to live under Iraq's government. Many Kurds became sick and hungry. The U.S. military joined with other countries to help the Kurds. The U.S. military used aircraft to deliver 25,000 pounds (11,340 kilograms) of food and supplies to them. CCTs provided air traffic control for these aircraft.

Tri-Crab '97

Combat Controllers must constantly train to stay in top physical condition. They also must practice their skills. CCTs often train with other USAF members. They sometimes train with members of other U.S. military branches. CCTs also hold training exercises with military members from other countries. These training missions help them learn new skills and practice teamwork.

Combat Controllers need to continually train to be prepared for their missions.

Tri-Crab '97 was a training exercise held on the U.S. island of Guam in 1997. U.S. Air Force, Navy, and Marine Corps members worked together during this exercise. They trained with naval groups from Australia and Singapore. Their training mission involved working with explosive devices. These troops also practiced rescue and first aid skills. CCTs provided communication support during the training.

Future of Combat Control

Some military leaders believe there will be no major wars in the future. They believe the United States may perform more special operations missions. Combat Controllers will be needed for these missions.

Today, the USAF does not have as many CCTs as it needs. Many people do not know about special forces jobs in the USAF. The USAF looks for ways to encourage men to enter CCT training.

Special Tactics and Rescue Specialists (STARS) helps people learn more about combat controllers. STARS is the AFSOC Parachute

Combat Controllers are needed for many special operations missions.

Demonstration Team. This is a group of CCTs and PJs who perform parachute jumps for the public. They perform during air shows, car races, and sports events. STARS members also talk to people about their jobs as combat controllers and pararescuemen.

Words to Know

altitude (AL-ti-tood)—the height of an object above the ground

assault zone (uh-SAWLT ZOHN)—an area in enemy territory where the military carries out a mission

beacon (BEE-kuhn)—light signal that helps pilots locate an assault zone

branch (BRANCH)—one part of a large group; the U.S. Air Force is one branch of the U.S. military.

communicate (kuh-MYOO-nuh-kate)—to share information with others

drop zone (DROP ZOHN)—an area set up for parachutists to land

equipment (i-KWIP-muhnt)—the tools and machinery needed to perform a task

landing zone (LAND-ing ZOHN)—a place Combat Controllers set up for aircraft to land

mission (MISH-uhn)—a military task

motto (MOT-oh)—a saying that describes what a group stands for; Combat Controllers' motto is "First There."

parachute (PA-ruh-shoot)—a piece of strong, light weight fabric used to drop people safely from aircraft

satellite radio (SAT-uh-lite RAY-dee-oh)—a radio that sends signals to spacecraft orbiting the earth

transport (transs-PORT)—to move people and supplies from one place to another

To Learn More

Blue, Rose and Corrine J. Naden. *The U.S. Air Force.* Defending Our Country. Brookfield, Conn.: Millbrook Press, 1993.

Bohrer, David. *America's Special Forces.* Osceola, Wis.: MBI Publishing, 1998.

Covert, Kim. *U.S. Air Force Special Forces: Pararescue.* Warfare and Weapons. Mankato, Minn.: Capstone Books, 2000.

Green, Michael. *The United States Air Force.* Serving Your Country. Mankato, Minn.: Capstone Books, 1998.

Useful Addresses

Air Force Public Affairs Office
1690 Air Force Pentagon
Washington, DC 20330-1690

Air Force Public Affairs Resource Library
1600 Air Force Pentagon
Washington, DC 20330-1690

Pararescue/Combat Control Selection Team
1780 Carswell Avenue, Suite 2
Lackland AFB, TX 78236-5506

United States Air Force Museum
1100 Spaatz Street
Wright-Patterson AFB
Dayton, OH 45433-7102

Internet Sites

Combat Control Pages
http://www.specialtactics.com/cctmain.html

USAF Combat Control
http://www.hurlburt.af.mil/stn/cct/index.html

**USAF STARS Parachute Demonstration
Team**
http://www.hurlburt.af.mil/stn/stars/index.html

Index